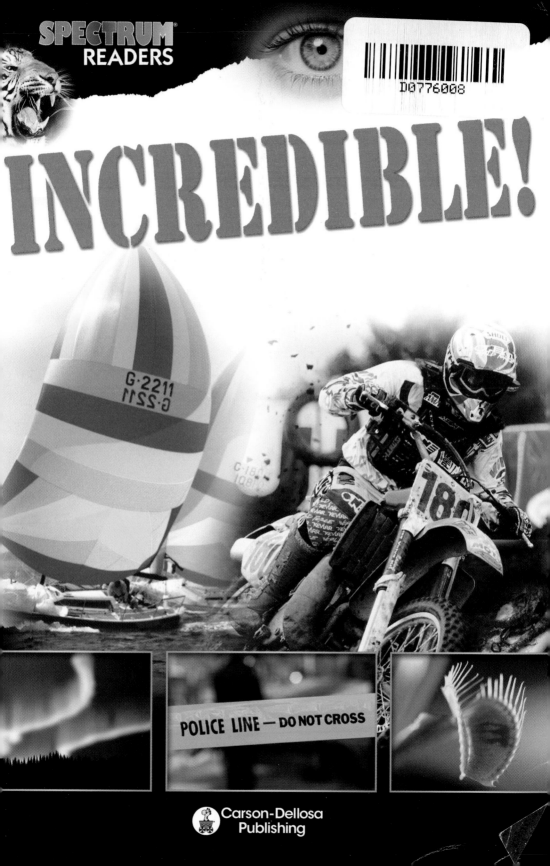

SPECTRUM READERS

INCREDIBLE!

D0776008

POLICE LINE — DO NOT CROSS

G·2211

Carson-Dellosa Publishing

SPECTRUM®

An imprint of Carson-Dellosa Publishing, LLC
P.O. Box 35665
Greensboro, NC 27425-5665

The publisher would like to thank the NOAA Photo Library, NOAA
Central Library; OAR/ERL/National Severe Storms Laboratory (NSSL)
for their permission to reproduce their photograph used on the cover,
title page and on pages 99 and 126 of this publication.

carsondellosa.com

Printed in the USA. All rights reserved.
ISBN 978-1-62399-160-9

02-146147784

Guided Reading Level: K

STOP!
Crime Scene

POLICE LINE — DO NOT CROSS

By Teresa Domnauer

Table of Contents

At the scene of a crime, there are clues.
A crime scene investigator must find the clues
that will help solve the crime.
Sometimes, the clues are easy to find.
Other times, the clues are not so clear.
Many different people help
an investigator along the way.

First Responder

The first responder is the first person
to arrive at a crime scene.
A crime scene is where a crime took place.
A police officer or a firefighter
might be the first responder.
An ambulance driver or any person
who was nearby could also be
the first responder.

Weird Facts

- If someone is hurt, the first responder
  might try to help him or her.

- A crime scene can be dangerous. The
  person who committed the crime may be
  there when the first responder arrives.

POLICE LINE — DO N

Secure the Crime Scene

After a crime happens,
it is important to secure the scene.
The police hang bright yellow tape
around the area where the crime happened.
This keeps people away from the scene.
It also keeps people from moving
or damaging the evidence, or clues.

Weird Facts

- Police keep track of who enters and exits a crime scene. Then, if something happens to the scene, they know who to question about it.

- A crime scene can be as small as a closet or as large as a football field.

Photographs

It is important to have photographs of the crime scene.
Sometimes, a police officer takes the photographs.
Sometimes, a crime scene photographer takes them.
They photograph every part of the scene.
Later, they can look at the crime scene again and again in the photographs.

Weird Facts

- A crime scene is often videotaped as well as photographed.
- Crime scene investigators take written notes about the crime scene, too.

The Search for Evidence

Investigators look for evidence all around
the crime scene.
They look for anything that will tell them
who committed the crime.
Evidence can be footprints, fingerprints,
blood, or bullets.
Computers, tools, cars, and weapons
can all be evidence, too.

Weird Facts

- Before searching for evidence, investigators
  draw a map of the crime scene.

- If a suspect—a person who might have
  committed the crime—leaves a footprint,
  investigators can make a copy of the print.

13

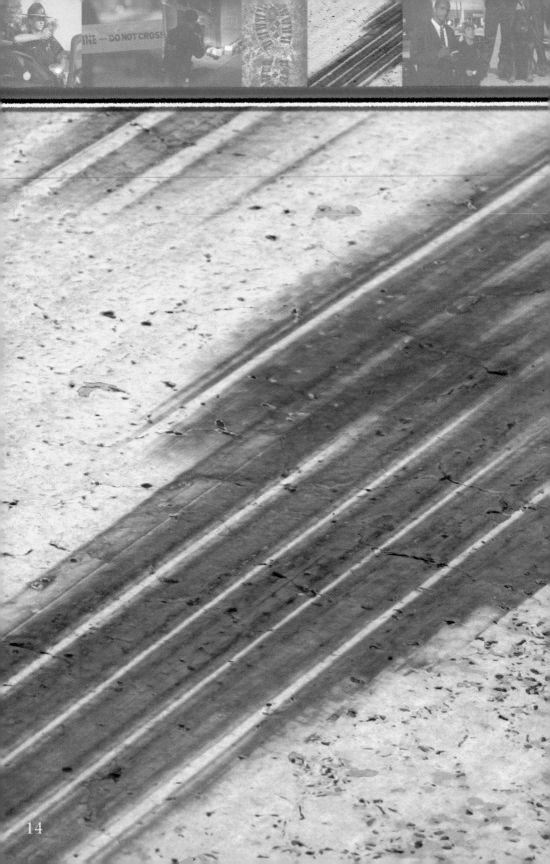

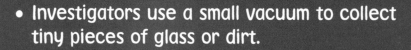

Sometimes, evidence is easy to see,
such as tire tracks.
Some evidence is harder to spot.
This evidence is called *trace evidence*.
Hairs, grains of sand, and threads
from clothing are all kinds of trace evidence.
Scientists examine this evidence
under a microscope.

Weird Facts

- Investigators use a small vacuum to collect tiny pieces of glass or dirt.

- Trace evidence can also be picked up with tweezers.

Police gather other kinds of evidence, too.
They talk to people who may have seen
the crime.
These people are called *witnesses*.
Police ask the witnesses questions
about what they saw and heard.
Any kind of information can be helpful
in solving the crime.

Weird Facts

- The police find out the names and addresses of all the witnesses of the crime.

- Witnesses are not allowed to talk to each other about the crime. They might confuse one another about what they saw or heard.

Special Experts

Sometimes, dogs help investigate crimes. Their strong sense of smell helps the police find people.

Dogs can also sniff out drugs and explosives. Police dogs go through special training to do this job.

- A dog has a sense of smell that is one million times greater than a human being's.

- Some dogs can follow trails of scent that are over an hour old.

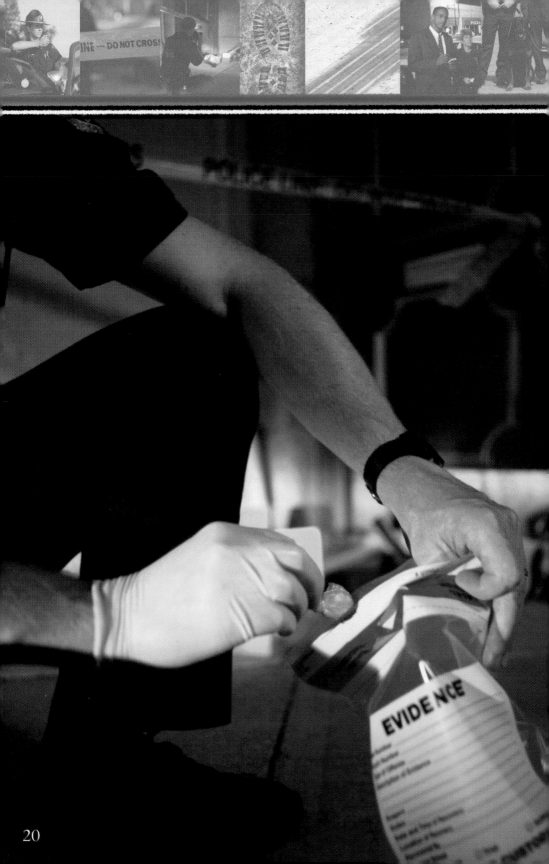

Recording Evidence

Investigators collect evidence very carefully.
They wear special gloves.
They place the objects in plastic bags
and bottles.
They label each item.
They try to keep evidence clean and pure
so that it can be used in court.
Investigators want the evidence to be
exactly how it was at the crime scene.

Weird Facts

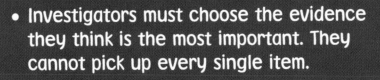

- Investigators must choose the evidence they think is the most important. They cannot pick up every single item.

- There must be a record of everything that happens to a piece of evidence.

21

Crime Lab

Investigators take evidence to the crime lab.
There, scientists try to find out more
about it.
They view blood or other chemicals
under a microscope.
The microscope lets scientists see
the tiniest of clues.

Weird Facts

- Scientists use special X-ray machines to look at evidence in the crime lab.

- The scientists who work in a crime lab are called *forensic scientists*.

23

Ballistics

Ballistics is the study of guns and bullets.
At the crime lab, experts in ballistics
look carefully at the marks on a bullet.
These marks are called *grooves*.
The grooves show an expert
which type of gun the bullet came from.

Weird Facts

- Ballistics experts can also tell the distance from which a gun was fired by looking at the bullet.

- Computers also help experts match bullets to guns.

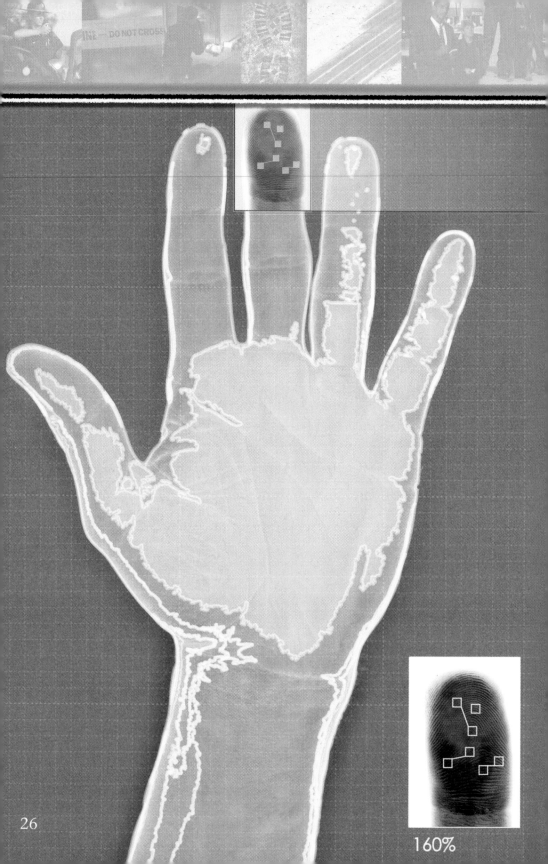

160%

Fingerprints

Sometimes, criminals leave fingerprints
at a crime scene.
It is an investigator's job to find them.
First, the investigator dusts the area
with a special powder.
Then, he or she lifts the prints with tape.
Computers search for prints that match
the ones from the crime scene.

Weird Facts

- No two people have the same fingerprints.
  Even identical twins have different
  fingerprints!

- A person's fingerprints do not change
  throughout his or her life.

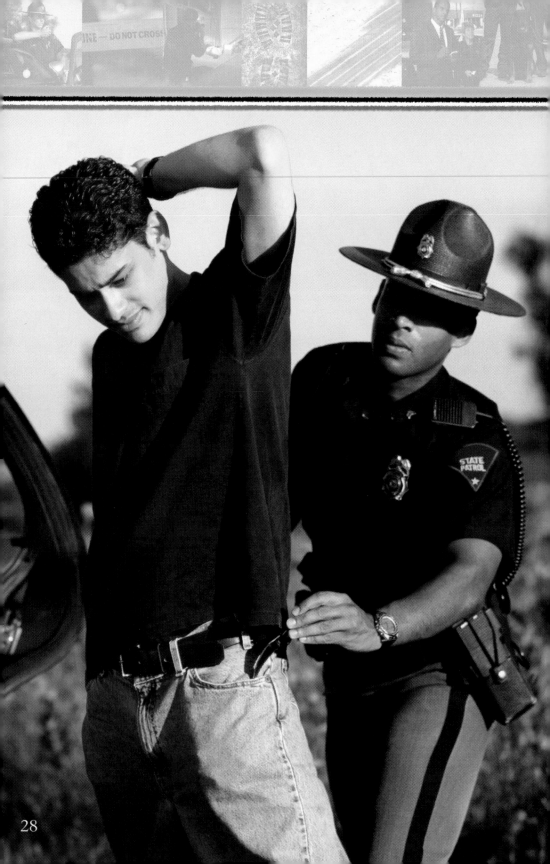

Suspect

If an investigator finds enough evidence, the police can arrest a suspect.
A suspect is a person whom the police think committed the crime.
A suspect is innocent until proven guilty in a court of law.

- A suspect in a serious crime may be held in jail until the trial.

- Sometimes, a suspect is placed in a police "lineup." Witnesses look at the lineup to see if they recognize anyone in it.

29

Detective Work

A detective is a type of investigator.
Police detectives are given
certain crimes to investigate.
They are always looking for more
information about their cases, or crimes.
They speak to many witnesses.
They ask suspects many questions.
They keep records of everything they do.

Weird Facts

- Detectives often visit places where the suspects might live or spend time.

- Crime scene investigations do not happen quickly. Some last for years and years.

Evidence in Court

Sometimes, a criminal case goes
to a court of law.
A group of people called a *jury* decides
if the suspect is innocent or guilty.
Sometimes, a judge decides.
The evidence is shown in the court.
The judge makes sure the evidence was
handled carefully.
Then, the judge makes a decision.

Weird Facts

- If evidence has not been handled carefully, the judge might not let it be used in court.

- In court, witnesses have a chance to tell what they saw happen at the crime scene.

STOP! Crime Scene Comprehension Questions

1. What is a crime scene?

2. Why is securing the crime scene important?

3. Why is it important to have photographs of a crime scene?

4. Do you think searching for evidence is easy or hard to do? Why?

5. Who is a witness?

6. How can dogs help investigate crimes? Why do you think a dog is better than a human for some jobs?

7. Why do you think investigators wear gloves when collecting evidence?

8. Who is a suspect?

9. What do you think happens to a suspect after he or she is arrested?

10. What is a jury? Do you think you would like to be on a jury?

INCREDIBLE!
Foods

By Teresa Domnauer

Table of Contents

People eat different kinds of foods.
In some countries,
people enjoy eating snails.
In other places, seaweed soup makes
a delicious breakfast.
All around the world, there are
weird and wonderful things to eat!

Snails

In France, snails are a special
thing to eat.
A dish made with snails is
called *escargot* (ess-car-GO).
To make escargot, the snails are
taken out of their shells.
Then, they are cooked
with butter and other ingredients.

Weird Facts

- In France, people eat thousands of tons of snails each year.

- Snails were among the first animals that people ate.

Caviar

Caviar is a food made from fish eggs.
The eggs come from fish called *sturgeon*.
Caviar is never cooked.
It is usually served on small pieces of
toast or with tiny pancakes called *blini*.
Fine caviar is very expensive.

Weird Facts

- Some of the world's best caviar comes from Russia and Iran.

- Caviar should not be served with a metal spoon. It changes the taste. Special spoons of bone or tortoise shell are used to serve caviar.

Sushi

Sushi is a kind of food
that comes from Japan.
It is usually made of rice wrapped
in seaweed.
Some sushi has raw fish in it.
Salmon and tuna are two kinds of fish
used in sushi.
Sushi is served with soy sauce
and a spicy green topping called
wasabi (WA-sah-bee).

Weird Facts

- Some chefs study for many years to become master sushi chefs.

- The word *sushi* does not mean "raw fish." It describes the sticky rice used in sushi that has been cooked in vinegar.

Oysters

Oysters are a kind of shellfish.
Often, they are eaten raw.
Raw oysters are served in their shells on ice.
Most people eat them with lemon
and a spicy sauce.
Oysters are wet and slippery.
They slide right down the throat!

Weird Facts

- Pearls are found inside some special oysters called *pearl oysters.*

- Many of the world's oyster farms are in the United States, South Korea, Japan, and France. People raise and sell oysters there.

46

Squid

A squid is a sea creature.
It is in the same animal family
as the octopus.
People all around the world eat squid.
Sometimes, squid is fried.
Other times, squid is cooked in
tomato sauce.
Squid is very chewy to eat.

Weird Facts

- Octopus is even chewier to eat than squid. It needs to cook for a long time to make it less chewy.

- A squid's arms and tentacles can be eaten, too!

47

Alligator

If you go to Louisiana in the southern United States, you can order alligator for lunch.
You can also buy alligator meat in the grocery store.
People use alligator in a kind of cooking called *Cajun*.
This type of cooking is very spicy.
People eat grilled alligator, fried alligator, and alligator stew!

Weird Facts

- Alligator does not taste fishy. It has a taste all its own. Some people say it tastes a little like chicken.

- Crocodile meat is also eaten in countries such as Singapore, India, and Australia.

Insects

It may seem strange to eat insects.
But people have eaten insects
for thousands of years.
In Singapore or Thailand,
people eat ants.
In parts of Africa and South America,
people eat caterpillars.

Weird Facts

- Most insects are good for you. They are very high in protein and low in fat.

- In Mexico, over 300 different kinds of insects are used as food.

Tripe

Tripe is food made from the lining
of a cow's stomach.
Many people think it is delicious.
People use tripe to make soups
and stews.
It is eaten in many places in Europe.
Tripe can be found in most grocery
stores in the United States, too.

Weird Facts

- Tripe is an ingredient in some kinds
  of hot dogs.
- Tripe can be found in a Mexican soup
  called *menudo*.

Ostrich Eggs

The ostrich is the largest
bird in the world.
Its eggs are the largest in the world, too.
An ostrich egg is about the size
of a football.
One ostrich egg can make
scrambled eggs for ten people!

Weird Facts

- It takes 20 chicken eggs to make the same amount of food that one ostrich egg makes.
- Ostrich eggs have such tough shells that people use hammers to crack them open!

Fungi

Fungi are kinds of plants
that do not need sunshine to grow.
Mushrooms are a kind of fungus
that people eat.
People eat mushrooms all around
the world.
They put mushrooms in salad,
on pizza, in soups, and much more.

Weird Facts

- Many wild mushrooms are not safe to eat. Only experts should pick them for eating.

- Truffles are another kind of fungus that people eat. They grow underground and must be sniffed out by dogs or pigs.

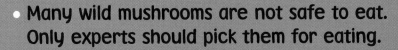

Flowers

Many people eat the seeds from flowers,
such as sunflower seeds.
But many people eat the flowers
themselves, too!
Flowers, such as marigolds, daisies,
and roses, can be eaten.
People put flowers in soups and salads.
People also use flowers to make tea.
Be careful, though, since not all flowers
are good or safe to eat.

Weird Facts

- Some flowers, such as violets, can be frosted with sugar and used to decorate cakes.

- People grow some vegetables, such as artichokes and broccoli, for their edible flowers.

Seaweed

Seaweed is a plant found in oceans
all around the world.
It can be used as food in many ways.
Japanese sushi is wrapped in
sheets of dried seaweed.
People in Hawaii and Asia eat
seaweed often.
They put it in soups and salads.
They also serve it with vegetables.

Weird Facts

- Seaweed is full of healthy vitamins and minerals.

- Seaweed is also used to make goods, such as toothpaste, paint, and soap.

Durian Fruit

This large, spiny fruit is a durian
(DUR-ee-en) fruit.
It grows on trees in Southeast Asia.
Many people think the durian fruit
is delicious.
But it has an awful smell!
People are not allowed to bring
durian fruit inside many hotels, taxis,
and airplanes.
This is because it smells so bad.

Weird Facts

- It can take as long as 15 years for a durian tree to grow fruit.

- The durian is one of the largest fruits in the world. It can weigh over ten pounds—as much as a bowling ball!

Food and Family

Food keeps people healthy and strong.
For many families around the world,
mealtime is a special part of the day.
It is a time when family members
can talk and relax together.
Families eat many different kinds
of food.
What kinds of food do you eat?

Weird Facts

- In South Africa, families eat puthu. Puthu is a kind of porridge made from corn.

- In India, families eat dal, a sauce made from lentils.

INCREDIBLE! Foods
Comprehension Questions

1. In which country are snails a special thing to eat?

2. What is caviar?

3. Name two kinds of fish used in sushi.

4. In which state can you have alligator for lunch?

5. What is tripe? What do people use tripe to make?

6. How big is an ostrich egg?

7. What fungus do many people eat in a salad or on a pizza?

8. What is seaweed? How is it eaten?

9. Why might you not be allowed to bring durian fruit on an airplane?

10. Which of these foods would you most like to eat? Which would you least like to eat?

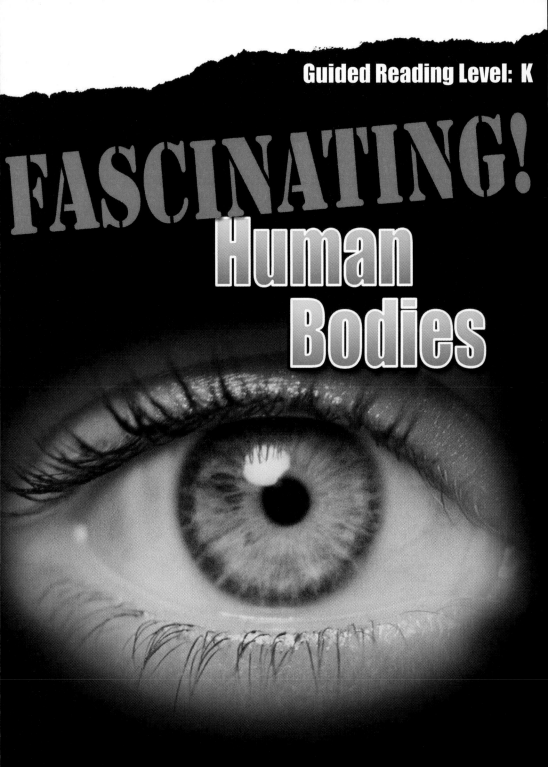

Guided Reading Level: K

FASCINATING!
Human
Bodies

By Katharine Kenah

Table of Contents

The human body
is a wonderful machine.
It can see and hear.
It can taste and touch.
It can run and jump.
It can think and dream.

The human body is beautiful,
surprising, and sometimes bizarre.

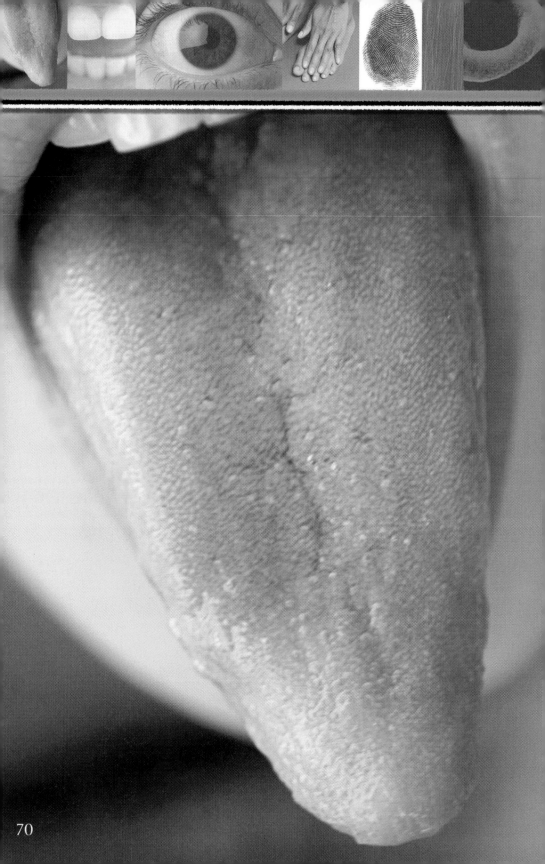

Tongue

Your tongue can change shape.
It moves around in your mouth.
This helps you eat and talk.
Tiny bumps on your tongue
are called *taste buds*.
They tell your brain when food
is sweet, sour, bitter, or salty.

- The tongue is one of the strongest muscles in the human body.

- The pattern of taste buds on your tongue is one of a kind. No one else has the same tongue print!

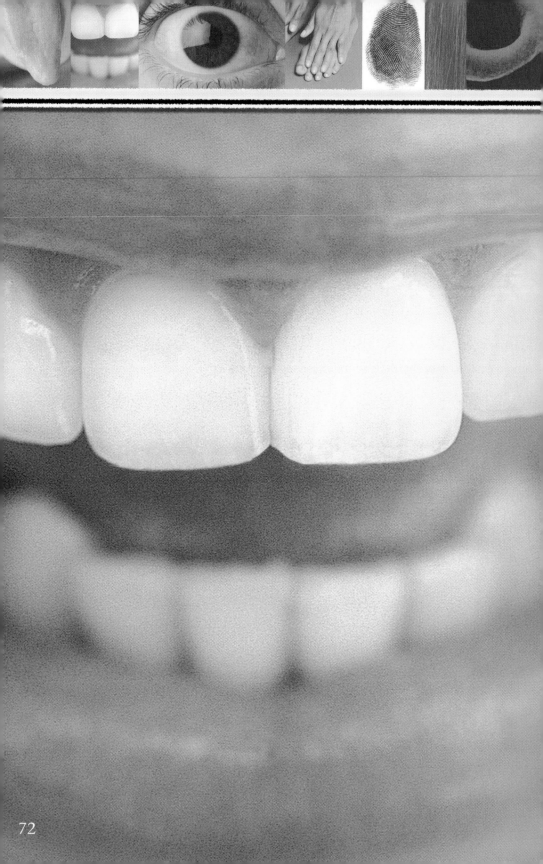

Teeth

You are born with two sets of teeth.
They are under your gums.
Twenty baby teeth grow in first.
They fall out one by one.
Later, thirty-two adult teeth grow in.
Different teeth have different jobs.
They work together to chew up food.

Weird Facts

- The hardest thing in the human body is tooth enamel.
- George Washington's false teeth were made of ivory and gold, not wood.

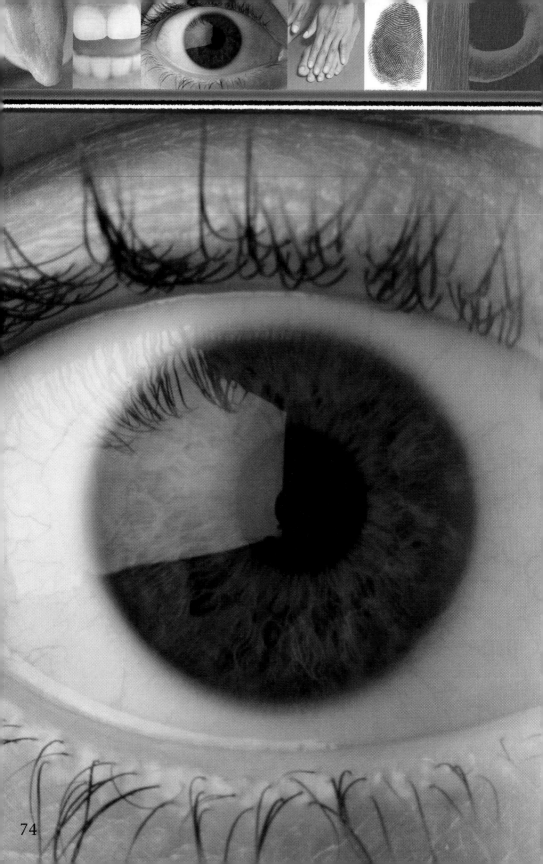

Eyes

Your eyes show you the world.
You use your eyes
for almost everything you do.
Eyeballs are only about one-inch wide.
They can see faraway things,
like stars, or things nearby, like flowers.
Your eyes cannot see anything
in total darkness.

Weird Facts

- If you lose sight in one eye, you lose only one-fifth of your vision. Your other eye will make up for some of the lost sight.

- Your eyes receive images upside down. Your brain turns them right-side-up before you "see" them.

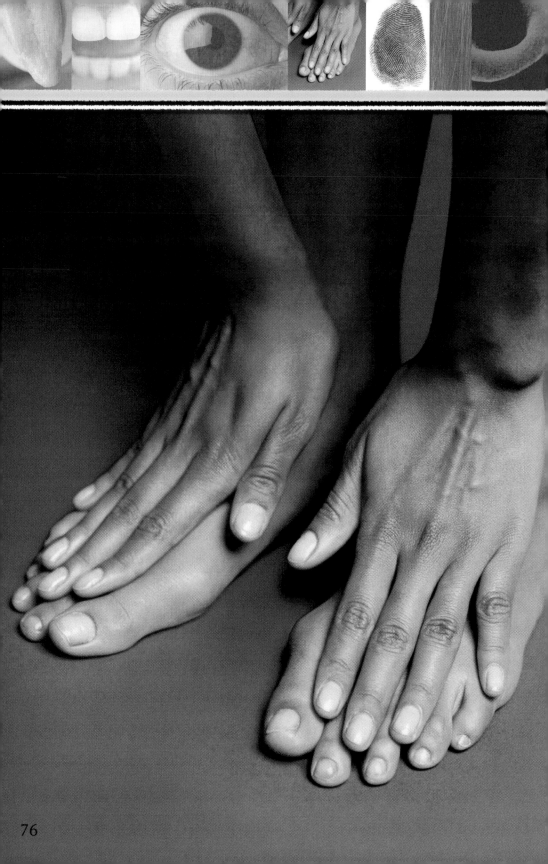

Fingernails and Toenails

Fingernails and toenails
are made from cells of hard skin.
They guard the ends of your
fingers and toes.
Nails grow from the base to the tip.
Each nail has a light half-moon shape
at its base.
Your nail starts to grow from this area.

Weird Facts

- Fingernails grow faster than toenails.
- It takes about six months for nails to grow from base to tip.

Fingerprint and Iris

Parts of your body are different
from everyone else's.
You have lines on the tips of your fingers.
These lines are called *fingerprints*.
No one else has your fingerprint.

The circle of color in your eye
is called the *iris*.
It controls light coming into the eye.
No one else has
an iris like yours.

Weird Facts

- If you hurt your fingertip, the skin will grow back with the same fingerprint!

- People with no color in their eyes are called *albinos*. Their irises are pinkish-gray.

Hair

Your hair is a lot like animals' fur.
It keeps your body warm.
Hair grows from tiny holes in your skin.
These holes are called *follicles*.
Straight hair grows out
of round follicles.
Curly hair grows out of flat follicles.
There are three million hairs
on the human body.

Weird Facts

- Beards have the fastest-growing hair. A beard could grow to be 30 feet long over a lifetime.

- People have hair on most parts of their bodies. They do not have hair on the palms of their hands, bottoms of feet, or lips.

81

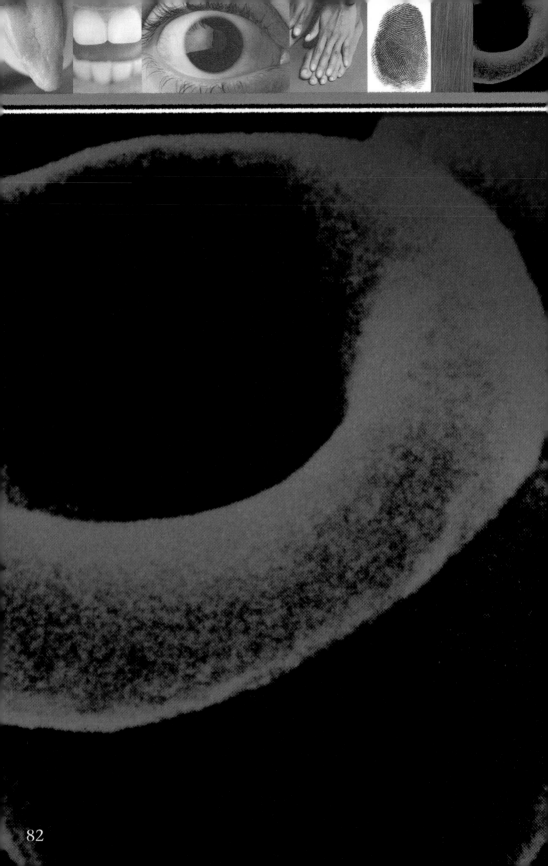

Blood

Blood works hard to keep you healthy.
It flows through the body in tubes.
They are called *vessels*.
Blood carries food throughout your body.
It carries oxygen to your cells.
It carries away waste that the body does
not need.

Weird Facts

- All people do not have the same kind of blood.
  Blood is sorted into four types—*A, B, AB,* and *O.*
  The most common blood type in the world is *O.*

- The average person has 30 billion
  red blood cells.

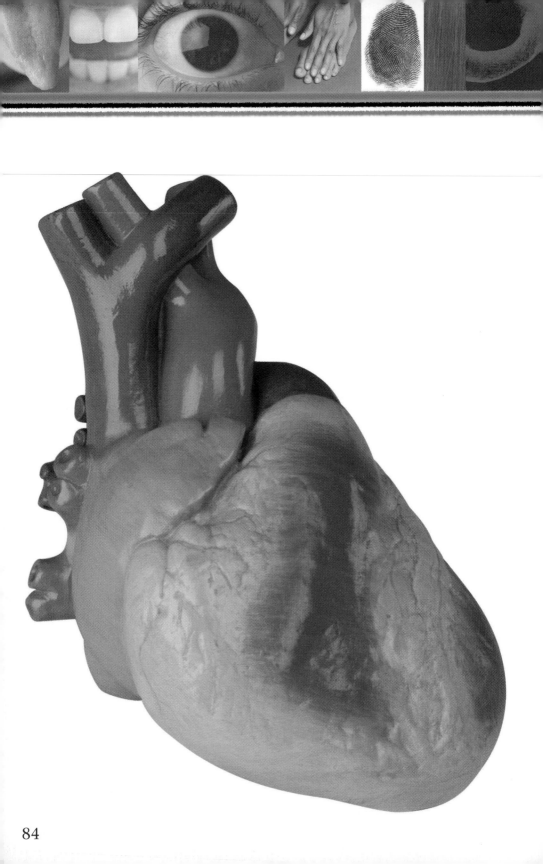

Heart

Your heart is made of special muscle.
It sends blood throughout the body.
The heart has two pumps.
One sends blood to your body.
One sends blood to your lungs.
It makes a pumping sound called a *heartbeat*.

Weird Facts

- A baby's heart beats faster than an adult's. A baby's heart beats 135 times a minute. An adult's heart beats about 70 times a minute.

- There are more heart attacks on Mondays than on any other day of the week.

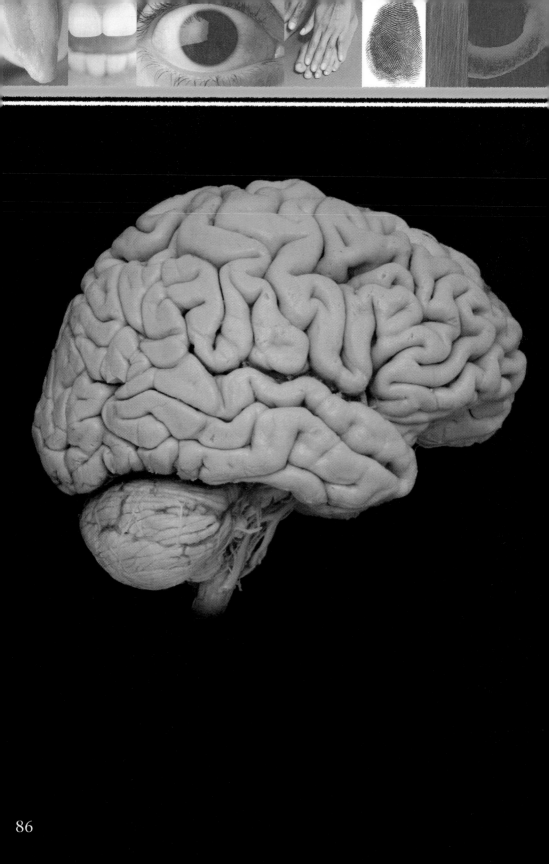

Brain

The brain is the control center
of your body.
It directs the way you think and act.
Your brain has two halves.
The right half controls
the left side of the body.
The left half controls
the right side of the body.
The brain is a grayish-pink color.
It weighs about three pounds.

Weird Facts

- The brain is made of nerve cells. Yet, it has no sensory nerves of its own. Your brain cannot feel pleasure or pain.

- The brain is wrinkled. This allows it to fit inside the skull.

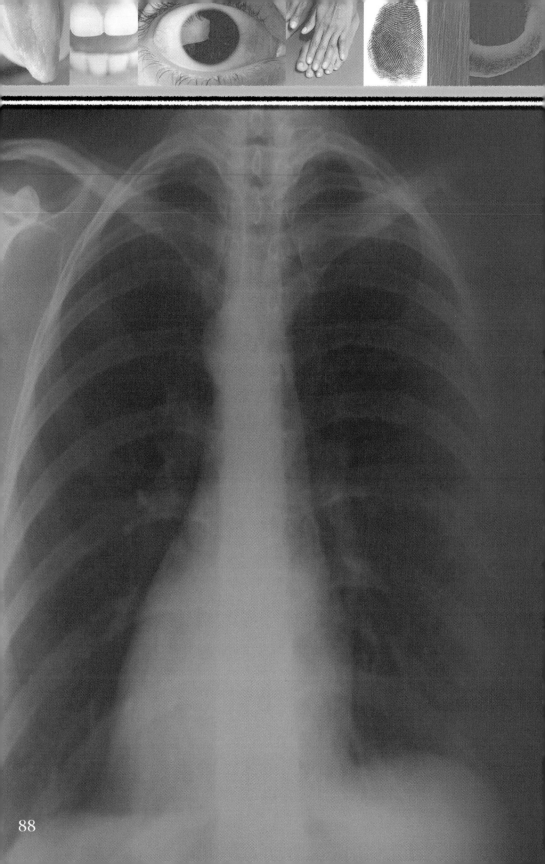

Lungs

Your lungs help you breathe.
They keep you alive.
The body cannot hold onto air
for a long time.
It always needs a new supply.
When you breathe in,
your lungs get bigger.
Air flows into your body.
Fresh air gives you power
to work and play.

Weird Facts

- No matter how hard you breathe out, you cannot force all the air out of your lungs.

- There are seven million alveoli, or tiny air sacs, in your lungs. If spread out flat, they could cover a tennis court.

89

Muscles

Your body has over 600 muscles.
These muscles work together.
They stretch and bend to help you move.
When muscles are used, they grow bigger.
Muscles also need rest, just like you.

Weird Facts

- You use muscles in your sleep. People change position about 35 times a night.
- Without muscles, your face would have no expression.

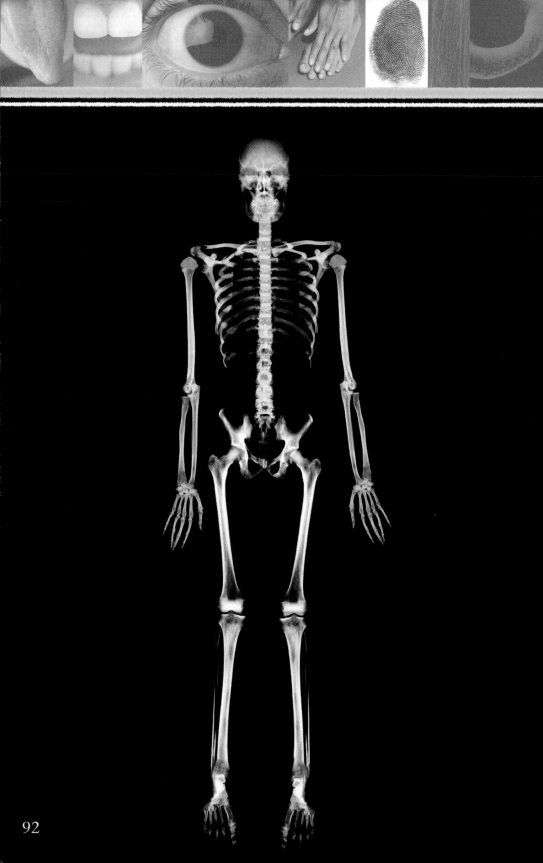

Skeleton

Walls give a house its shape.
The skeleton gives your body its shape.
There are 206 bones in the skeleton.
They guard your heart, brain, and lungs.
When two bones come together,
they form a joint.
Joints let you bend, walk, and run.

Weird Facts

- Almost 25 percent of your bones are in your feet!

- Babies are born with 300 bones. Adults have 206 bones. As you grow, some bones join together.

93

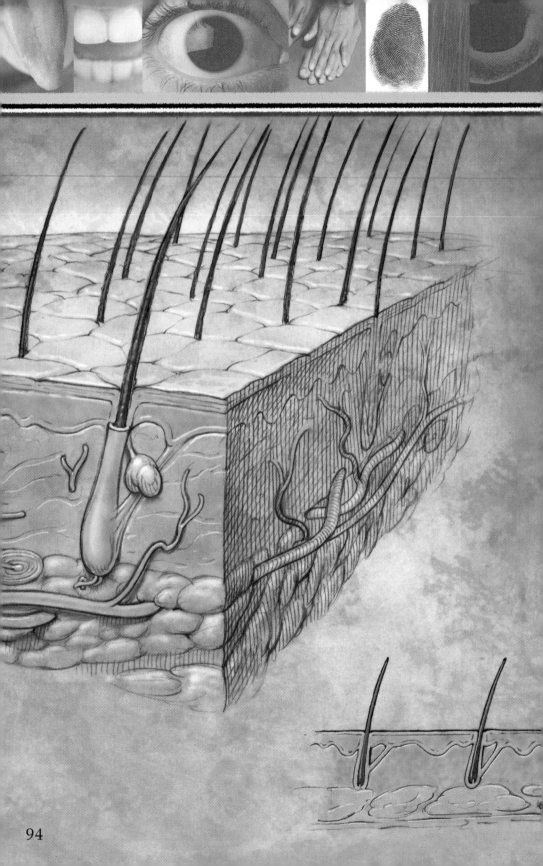

Skin

Your skin is the largest organ
in your body.
It helps you stay healthy.
Your skin keeps out dirt and germs.
It keeps in body fluids.
It also keeps your body from getting
too warm or too cold.
New skin grows all the time.

Weird Facts

- Every hour, a person loses about 600,000 skin cells.

- There are 45 miles of nerves in your skin.

Excuse Me!

Sometimes, your body is surprising.
A hiccup is a sudden intake of air.
The longest case of hiccups on record lasted
69 years!
A sneeze is a sudden rush of air out of the
nose and mouth.
It can travel over 100 miles per hour.
When you have too much gas in
your stomach, it must come out.
Most people release a pint of intestinal gas
a day!

Weird Facts

- In a lifetime, a person produces enough spit to fill two swimming pools.

- A snore can be almost as loud as a power drill.

FASCINATING! Human Bodies Comprehension Questions

1. Name at least five things a human body can do.

2. What does your tongue help you do?

3. What do taste buds do?

4. How many baby teeth do people have? How many adult teeth do people have?

5. How wide are your eyeballs?

6. What is the job of fingernails and toenails?

7. What two parts of your body are different from everyone else's?

8. What are *follicles*?

9. How many hairs are on the human body?

10. What does the right half of your brain control? What does the left half control?

11. How many muscles are in your body?

MYSTERIOUS!
Outer Space

Table of Contents

Most people wake
up with the Sun.
They go to sleep
looking at the Moon.

Every day, the sky affects
our lives in big and small ways.
Turn the page and step outside.
The mysteries of space are
waiting for you!

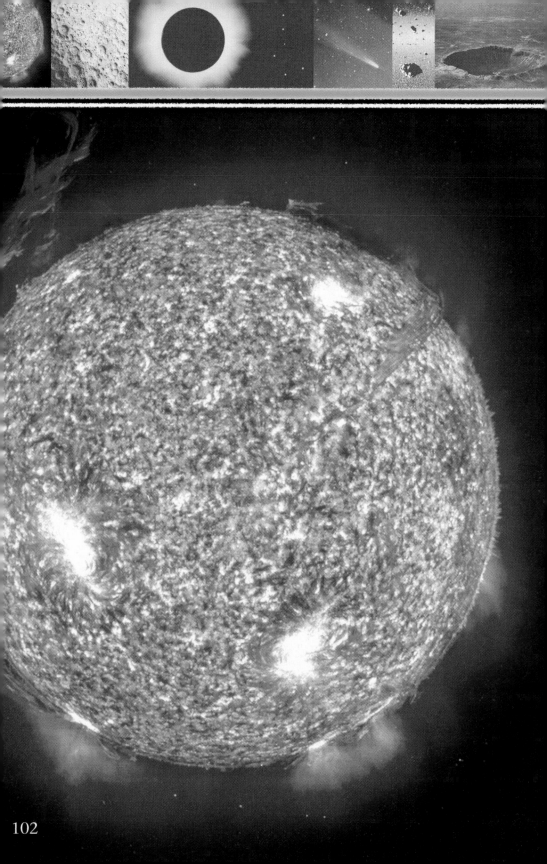

Sun

The Sun is not a big star.
It is not a small star.
It is just an average-sized star.
But it is the star closest to Earth.

The Sun is a ball of hot, burning gas.
It sends heat, light, and energy
to people, plants, and animals.
There would be no life on Earth
without the Sun.

Weird Facts

- The temperature at the Sun's center is 26 million degrees.
- The Sun is 110 times larger than Earth.

Moon

The Moon is Earth's
closest neighbor in space.
It is made of rock.
The Moon has no weather,
no wind, and no water.

The Moon is the brightest light
in the night sky.
But the Moon makes
no light of its own.
Moonlight is sunlight that
bounces off the Moon!

Weird Facts

- Moon dust is made of ground rock and glass.

- If Earth were the size of a basketball, the Moon would be the size of a tennis ball.

Eclipse

Earth circles the Sun.
The Moon circles Earth.

Sometimes, the Moon passes
between the Sun and Earth.
The light of the Sun
is hidden by the Moon.
This is called a *solar eclipse*.

Sometimes, Earth passes
between the Sun and the Moon.
Earth's shadow covers the moon.
This is called a *lunar eclipse*.

Weird Facts

- A solar eclipse can be seen only in places where the Moon's shadow covers the ground.

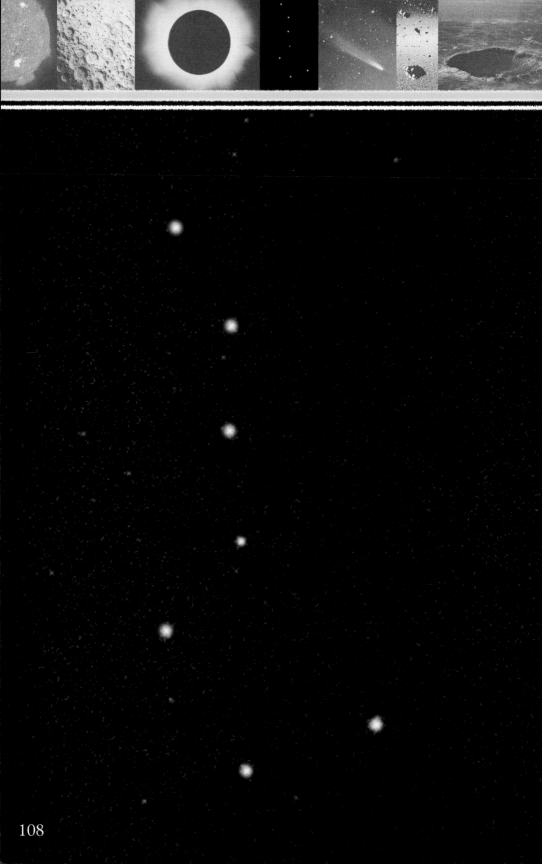

Constellations

Some stars form pictures
or shapes in the night sky.
These groups of stars
are called *constellations*.
Constellations are named for animals,
people in myths, and everyday things.

Weird Facts

- The Big Dipper looks like a soup ladle.
  The two stars at the far end of the ladle
  point to the North Star.

- The North Star, or the Polaris Star, is
  right above the North Pole.

Comet

A comet is like a giant,
dirty snowball.
It is more than a mile wide.
A comet is made of dust,
rocks, gas, and ice.

Comets move around the Sun.
The Sun's heat melts some
of the comet's icy outside.
Dust and gas fly out into space.
This forms the comet's bright tail.

Weird Facts

- Halley's Comet is a comet that appears in the sky every 76 years. It was named after Edmund Halley.

- Shooting stars are bits of comet dust and ice falling into Earth's atmosphere.

Asteroid

An asteroid is a lump of rock.
It looks like a potato.
Some asteroids are tiny. Some are huge.
The asteroid Ceres is 620 miles across!

Most asteroids move around the Sun
between Mars and Jupiter.
This area is called the *asteroid belt*.
Asteroids are as old as the solar system.
They may be pieces of planets
that never formed.

Weird Facts

- Asteroids are full of valuable metals, such as nickel and iron. Mining companies are working on ways to mine these metals in space!

- Near Earth Asteroids are asteroids that pass close to Earth. A collision with these asteroids could cause disaster.

Meteoroids

Small objects falling through space
are called *meteoroids*.
Meteoroids are made of bits of rock
from crashing asteroids.
They are also made of dust
falling from comets.

When meteoroids hit the air
around Earth, they get hot and glow!
These streaks of lights are called *meteors*.
If a meteoroid lands on Earth,
it is called a *meteorite*.

Weird Facts

- Some people think that a meteorite crash 65 million years ago may have killed the dinosaurs on Earth.

- 50,000 years ago, a million-ton meteorite hit Arizona. It made a bowl-shaped dent in the ground. The crater is 570 feet deep and nearly a mile wide!

Milky Way

The Milky Way is a galaxy.
A galaxy is a group of stars
spinning in space.
Every star in the universe is in a galaxy.

The Milky Way is shaped
like a pinwheel. It is made of
billions of stars, dust clouds, and gas.
Our solar system is just one small part
of this huge galaxy.

Weird Facts

- The Milky Way is shaped like a pancake with a thick center and thin edges.
- The Milky Way has dark spots that look like holes. They are really just dust clouds that hide the stars behind them.

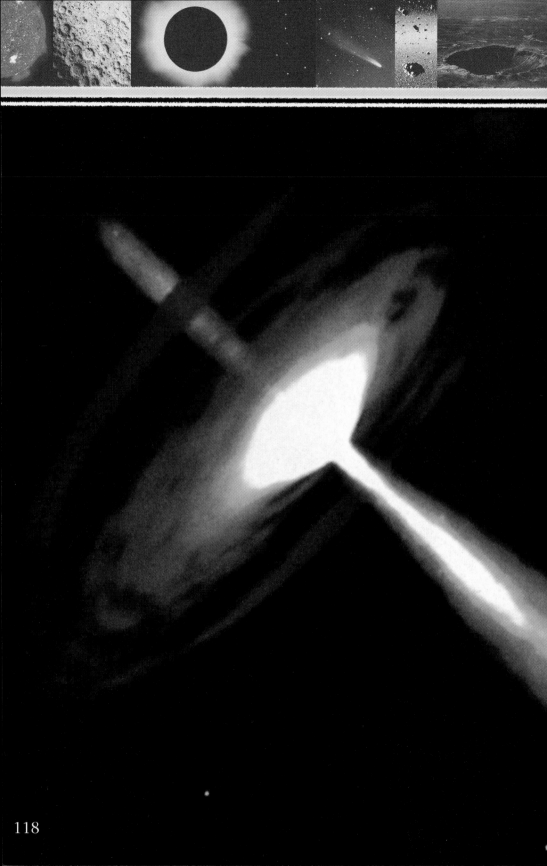

Black Hole

This is not a top spinning in space.
It is a black hole!

When people jump into the air, a force
called *gravity* pulls them back down.
A black hole is a spot in space
where gravity is very strong!
A black hole pulls everything into it.
Nothing can escape it, not even light.

Weird Facts

- A black hole cannot be seen by the human eye.
- Temperatures near the edge of a black hole rise close to 180 million degrees!

119

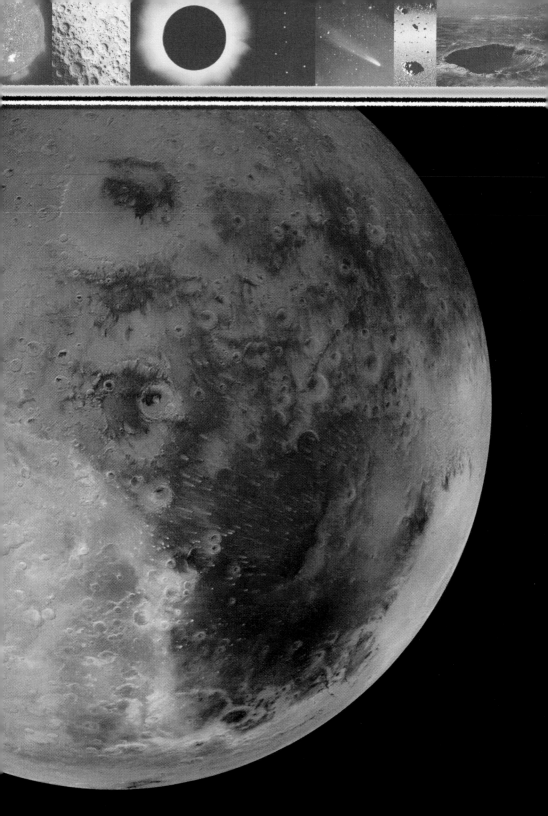

Mars

Mars is called the *Red Planet*.
Mars' red color comes from
the iron in its soil.
Mars has mountains, deserts,
canyons, and polar ice caps just like Earth.
But Mars has no water to drink
and no oxygen to breathe.
Huge wind and dust storms
whirl around Mars.

Weird Facts

- Mars has weaker gravity than Earth. If you weighed 100 pounds on Earth, you'd weigh 40 pounds on Mars.

- Mars got its name from the god of war in ancient myths.

121

Saturn

Saturn is the second largest planet
in our solar system.
It is full of liquid.
This makes Saturn very light.
It would float on water!

Saturn has seven rings.
Saturn's rings are made of
chunks of rock and ice.
These chunks can be as small as
snowflakes or as big as houses!

Weird Facts

- Saturn has "shepherd moons." These
  moons keep chunks of rock and ice in the
  rings from straying out of place, just like
  a shepherd keeps sheep together.

Dwarf and Giant Stars

A star lives in space for
millions of years. It shines
until it runs out of fuel.
Then, the star starts to swell.
It grows to 30 times its normal size.
This is called a *red giant*.

Then, the star puffs out gas and dust.
It starts to shrink.
All that is left is the star's
tiny, hot center.
This is called a *white dwarf*.

Weird Facts

- The planetary nebula, or glowing part, of a dying star sometimes becomes part of a new star!

Northern Lights

Something is shimmering
in the sky. It looks like
a dancing curtain of lights.
Is it lightning? Is it a fire?
No! It is the northern lights.

Sometimes, small bits of gas
fly off from the Sun in streams.
They hit the air around Earth
and start to glow!
This is called the *northern lights*.

Weird Facts

- In the northern hemisphere, the northern lights are called the *aurora borealis*. In the southern hemisphere, they are called the *aurora australis*.

Sky Watching

When the Sun goes down,
sky watchers go outside.
Some people use telescopes.
Some people use binoculars.
Some people go to planetariums
to watch star shows.
Some people simply
use their own eyes.

Look carefully. The mysteries
of space are everywhere!

Weird Facts

- Ancient astronomers thought that the stars traveled around Earth.
- Laika was the first dog to explore space! Laika traveled into space in 1957 on board the Sputnik 2 satellite.

129

MYSTERIOUS! Outer Space Comprehension Questions

1. What star is closest to Earth?

2. Why do you think there would be no life on Earth without the Sun?

3. What is the moon made of? What is moonlight?

4. What is the difference between a solar eclipse and a lunar eclipse?

5. What are constellations? How are constellations named?

6. What is a comet made of?

7. Where is the asteroid belt? How big is the asteroid Ceres?

8. What are meteoroids made of? What is it called if a meteoroid lands on Earth?

9. Why do you think Mars is called the *Red Planet*?

10. How many rings does Saturn have? What are the rings made of?

11. Why do you think some people enjoy sky watching? Do you think it is something you

STRANGE!
Plants

Table of Contents

Imagine a world without plants.
There would be no vegetables to eat.
There would be no wooden houses
to live in.
Without plants, there would be no
life on earth.

Plants are everywhere.
Some plants are big.
Some plants are small.
Some plants are weird and wacky!

Bird-of-Paradise

Is that a bird? No, it is a plant!
The bird-of-paradise is named after
its bright orange and blue flower.
The flower looks like the head of a bird.
This plant is native to South Africa.
A giant form of it grows in the state
of Hawaii in the United States.

Weird Facts

- Bird-of-paradise plants look like the flying birds-of-paradise, which are brightly colored birds.

- Seeds of the bird-of-paradise are poisonous if eaten.

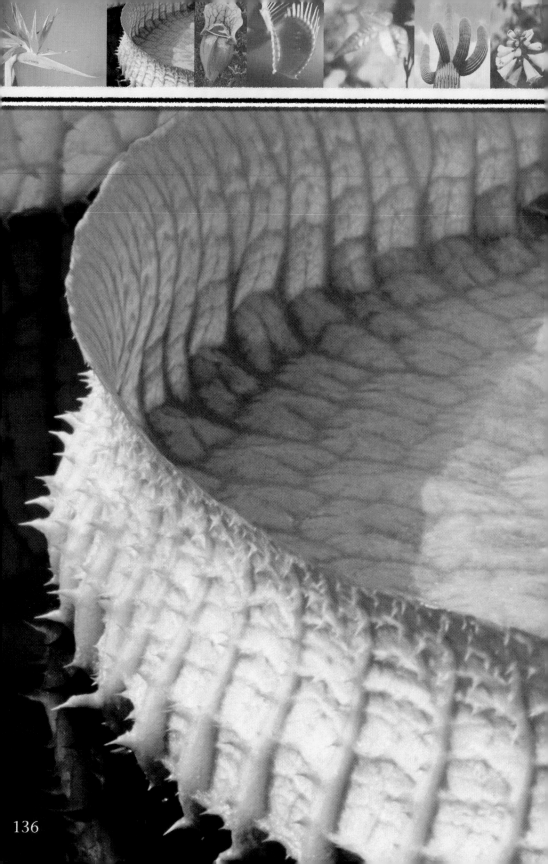

Giant Water Lily

The largest water lily in the world
is the giant water lily.
Its round leaves are seven feet wide.
A person could lie down inside of one!
The giant water lily grows in the
warm waters of the Amazon River.
This river is in South America.

Weird Facts

- The giant water lily is also called the *Victoria amazonica*. It was named in 1838 after Queen Victoria of England.

- A giant water lily's flowers smell like butterscotch and pineapple.

Pitcher Plant

A pitcher plant is a death trap for bugs.
It smells sweet.
The red stripes make it look like meat.
A bug flies to the plant looking for a meal.
The inside is slippery and covered
with sharp hairs.
When a bug falls inside, it cannot get out.

Weird Facts

- Pitcher plants have a drug in them that makes bugs unsteady. Bugs wobble along the rims of the plants. Then, they fall down into these deadly traps.

- Pitcher plants have clear spots on them. Bugs fly toward these sunny "windows" to escape. But they crash into the leaf and fall into the belly of the plant.

Venus Flytrap

A fly lands on leaves that look like
an open mouth.
Snap! The leaves close.
The Venus flytrap has just trapped its food.
This plant has small hairs on its leaves.
The hairs sense when something is there.
The edges of the leaves lock to keep
bugs inside.

Weird Facts

- Venus flytraps snap shut in one-third of a second.

- It takes a Venus flytrap 8–20 days to eat a whole bug.

Poison Ivy

Do not touch these leaves.
They are poison ivy.
Poison ivy vines climb trees,
walls, and fences.
Poison ivy also forms into a bush.
Each leaf is made of three smaller leaves.
In spring, poison ivy leaves are red.
In summer, the leaves turn
shiny and green.

Weird Facts

- The leaves of poison ivy are poisonous all year long. Touching these leaves causes red, itchy bumps.

- An allergy to poison ivy is the most common one in the United States.

143

Saguaro Cactus

The saguaro is the largest cactus
in the United States.
It can grow to be 60 feet tall—
as tall as a six-story building.
A saguaro cactus grows in hot, dry deserts.
Its tall trunk and branches store water.
Sharp pins, called *spines*, cover
the saguaro cactus.

Weird Facts

- Some saguaro cacti are over 200 years old.
- Saguaro cacti can weigh ten tons—more than a school bus.

Foxglove

The foxglove gets its name from its flowers.
They are shaped like the fingers of a glove.
This purple plant looks pretty,
but it can cause harm.
A strong heart medicine is made
from foxglove leaves.
A small amount of this drug is good.
Too much of this drug can stop a heart!

Weird Facts

- Some tales say that fairies wore foxglove blossoms as gloves. Others say that foxes put them on their paws so that they could move quietly.

- All of the foxglove plant is poisonous if eaten.

Bamboo

Bamboo is giant grass with a strong stem.
Bamboo shoots grow close together
and very quickly.
Some grow three feet in one day!
Bamboo is used to make things,
like houses, shoes, fishing poles, rope,
and paper.

Weird Facts

- Layers of bamboo together are almost as strong as steel.

- Scientists think that bamboo is one of the world's earliest forms of grass.

Giant Sequoia

A giant sequoia is one of the biggest
and oldest living things on the earth.
It is a type of redwood tree.
The giant sequoia has a very large trunk.
Most trunks are 100 feet around.
It would take a circle of almost twenty
people holding hands to surround this
giant tree!

Weird Facts

- Giant sequoias live for thousands of years.
- The largest tree in the world is a sequoia called the *General Sherman Tree*. It is over 274 feet tall and 102 feet around. It is almost five times taller than an adult oak tree.

Lichen

A lichen is a plant with no leaves,
roots, flowers, or stems.
It can live in the deep Arctic cold.
It can live in the hot desert heat.
It can live and grow on a rock!
A lichen is made of both algae and fungi.
Algae help the lichen make food.
Fungi hold water for the lichen.

Weird Facts

- Slow-growing lichens can live to be 4,000 years old.

- For 2,000 years, doctors have used drugs made from lichens to treat lung and skin problems.

Kelp

Kelp is a large brownish-green seaweed
that grows underwater.
It is found in cold waters around the world.
Many sea animals use kelp
for food or shelter.
Giant kelp grows very long
and very quickly.
It can grow over 300 feet in one year!

Weird Facts

- A lot of giant kelp living together forms
  a kelp forest. There are no trees in
  this forest, just kelp!

- Algin, made from kelp, is used to make ice
  cream, paper, and toothpaste.

155

Cattail

Is that a cat hiding in the grass?
No, it is a cattail!
A cattail is a wild plant.
It lives along the edges
of ponds and lakes.
It has tall, pointy green leaves.
In the spring, a cattail has
a greenish-yellow flower.
By the end of summer, the flower is long,
dark, and fuzzy like a cat's tail.

Weird Facts

- Part of the cattail flower was once used to make silk. It is still used to make bandages for cuts.

- In some parts of the world, cattails are covered with oil and set on fire. They are used as lights. 157

Dandelion

A bright yellow dandelion
blooms all year long.
It opens during the day
and closes up at night.
A full-grown dandelion
has white, fluffy seeds.
The word *dandelion* means
"tooth of the lion."
People think the edges of its leaves look
like a row of lion's teeth.

Weird Facts

- The early colonists brought dandelion seeds to North America. They grew dandelions for food and medicine.

- Dandelions are edible weeds! They can be cooked or used in salads.

Orchid

Many gardeners think the orchid is
the most beautiful flower in the world.
It grows in every color except blue!
In warm places, an orchid will grow
in a tree.
In cool places, an orchid grows
on the ground.
Orchids are found in almost every type of
climate except deserts.

Weird Facts

- The vanilla vine is a climbing orchid. It
  produces pods called *vanilla beans*. The
  vanilla is used in drinks and foods.

- It takes some orchid plants up to four years
  to recover after producing a flower.

STRANGE! Plants
Comprehension Questions

1. Why are plants important?

2. Why do you think the bird-of-paradise was given its name?

3. Where might you find a giant water lily?

4. Why can bugs not get out of a pitcher plant after they fall inside?

5. What color are poison ivy leaves in the spring? What color are they in the summer?

6. What is the largest cactus in the United States? How tall can it grow?

7. How can the foxglove cause harm?

8. What is bamboo used for?

9. What is a lichen? Where can it be found?

10. What is kelp? How much can kelp grow in one year?

11. Why do you think the cattail was given its name?

RUN!
Predators

Table of Contents

Have you ever seen a bear
with a shopping cart?
Wild animals must find
their own food in the wild.

Some animals catch and eat
other living things.
These animals are called *predators*.

Predators hunt to stay alive.
Food gives them energy to live.

Alligator

The alligator moves closer.
Snap! It swallows the turtle whole.

Alligators are fast.
They have lots of sharp teeth.
They use their teeth to attack.
They do not use their teeth to chew.

Weird Facts

- Alligators have brains the size of hot dogs.
- Clear third eyelids help alligators see underwater.

Bald Eagle

A bald eagle flies on the wind.
It spreads its huge wings.
Suddenly, the eagle drops from the sky.
It grabs a fish with its feet.

Eagles are good hunters.
Eagles can see farther and better
than any other animal!
Their long, sharp claws
are called *talons*.

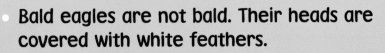

Weird Facts

- Bald eagles are not bald. Their heads are covered with white feathers.

- The bald eagle is the national bird of the United States.

Barracuda

A barracuda is called
the "tiger of the sea."
It has long jaws and sharp teeth.
Watch out! It eats quickly!

Barracudas eat other fish.
They live in warm, tropical water
near coral reefs and sunken ships.

Weird Facts

- Barracudas can be poisonous if they eat smaller fish that have eaten poisonous marine plants.

- Barracudas can weigh over 100 pounds, about the weight of a very large dog.

Polar Bear

A polar bear is hunting on the ice.
Its thick fur keeps it warm.

Creamy white fur makes
polar bears hard to see.
When a seal pops up for air,
this polar bear will pounce on it!

Weird Facts

- Polar bears can smell food up to 10 miles away. They can sniff seal dens under 3 feet of ice and snow.

- Some polar bears weigh more than 1,000 pounds. This is about the weight of a horse.

173

Komodo Dragon

The world's biggest lizard
is looking for a meal. *Flick!*
It smells the air with its tongue.

Komodo dragons never get lost.
They follow smells on the ground
to find their way.
Their bites poison the blood
of their victims.

Weird Facts

- Komodo dragons have third eyes on the tops of their heads. These eyes sense light.
- Komodo dragons may have inspired mythical dragons. They both have long necks, lashing tongues and tails, and sharp teeth.

175

Gray Wolf

A gray wolf licks its lips.
It watches its prey, waiting to attack.
Gray wolves hunt sick or weak animals.

Gray wolves live in packs
with other wolves.
The wolves protect each other.
The howls of gray wolves can be
heard 10 miles away!

Weird Facts

- Wolves are part of the dog family. They are the largest wild dogs in the world.

- Ancient people may have learned how to hunt by watching wolves hunt in packs.

Tasmanian Devil

This Tasmanian devil is jumping,
trying to look big and mean.
Its pink ears turn deep red.
A Tasmanian devil does not want
to share food.

Tasmanian devils are marsupials.
They carry their babies in pouches.
Tasmanian devils sleep during the day.
They hunt at night.

Weird Facts

- Tasmanian devils' jaws and teeth are very strong. They can eat every bit of their prey. They can even eat the bones!

Spitting Cobra

This spitting cobra senses danger.
It rears back. Its neck flattens.
Now, the cobra is ready to spit
venom into its victim's eyes.

Cobra poison is strong.
Bites bring death within hours.
Baby cobras can bite as soon as
they hatch from their eggs.

Weird Facts

- One tablespoon of dried venom could kill **165** people.
- Spitting cobras can move forward with their heads raised and their bodies still coiled-up.

Cheetah

Whoosh! Is it a rocket or a race car?
No, it is a cheetah!
A cheetah is the world's fastest
mammal on land.

Cheetahs can leap 23 feet in one bound.
They can run at 70 miles per hour,
as fast as a car.
Cheetahs need to cool down in the grass.

Weird Facts

- Cheetahs can go from 0 to 40 miles per hour in 2 seconds!

- Cheetahs' claws provide good traction because they do not retract. Their claws are always out.

Great White Shark

A great white shark
shoots through the water.
Its eyes roll back.
Its mouth opens wide, showing
seven rows of shiny white teeth.

Great white sharks are the
perfect killing machines.
They weigh more than most trucks.
They hear better than human beings.

Weird Facts

- Great white sharks are not all white. Their bodies are bluish-gray. Their bellies are white.

- Scientists believe these sharks have poor vision.

Brown Bear

A salmon swims *up* a waterfall.
Chomp! It is caught by a large and
powerful predator, the brown bear.
The brown bear hunts with its
strong jaws and huge paws.

Most animals walk on their toes.
Brown bears walk like people!
Each foot fully touches the ground
with each step.

Weird Facts

- Brown bears can run 25 miles per hour, as fast as an Olympic sprinter.

- Some brown bears weigh up to 1,700 pounds, as much as a car!

Badger

Do not let this sweet face fool you.
This short, furry creature
is a fierce fighter.
A badger has a pointed snout.
It hunts for food under leaves.

Badgers have long claws
for digging quickly!
They dig for food.
They also dig burrows to live in.

Weird Facts

- Snake venom only harms badgers if they are bitten on their noses.

- Badger fur is used to make paintbrushes.

Osprey

A fish wiggles to get away.
It is too late.
An osprey holds it in its claws.
The osprey's feet have tiny spikes.
The spikes help keep prey
from slipping away.

Ospreys build the biggest nests
of all the birds in North America.
They build them with sticks, seaweed,
and bones.
Some nests are 6 feet tall—
the size of a person!

Weird Facts

- Ospreys can plunge into water from high in the sky.

- Osprey nests can be seen for miles, perched atop trees, rocks, and poles.

191

Bengal Tiger

A Bengal tiger is the biggest
cat in the world.
It is very strong.
A Bengal tiger can live anywhere
that has food, shade, and water.

Bengal tigers can jump ten times
their length. They hunt at night.
Tiger stripes are like human fingerprints.
Every tiger has a different pattern.

Weird Facts

- Tigers' tongues are covered with spines for carrying water and combing the tigers' fur.

- Tigers attack from behind. Field workers wear masks of faces on the backs of their heads. This fools the tigers and prevents attacks.

193

RUN! Predators
Comprehension Questions

1. Why do predators hunt?

2. Why do alligators need a third eyelid?

3. Why do you think the bald eagle was given its name?

4. Why do you think the barracuda is called the "tiger of the sea"?

5. What does the komodo dragon use to smell?

6. Why do gray wolves live in packs?

7. What are marsupials? Do you know of any other animals, besides the Tasmanian devil, that are marsupials?

8. How fast can a cheetah run?

9. How are brown bears similar to people?

10. What do ospreys use to build their nests? Name one interesting thing about an osprey nest.

ULTIMATE!
Races

Table of Contents

Races are competitions of speed, strength, and skill.
Snowboard racers zoom down mountains.
Bicycle racers pedal into the wind.
Motocross racers fly through the mud.
They all want to be the first to finish.

Marathon

A marathon is a race that people run
on foot.
The race is 26.2 miles long!
Runners must pace themselves.
They don't want to run out of energy
before the race is over.
Runners train for months and months
to get ready for a marathon.

Weird Facts

- The Boston Marathon in Massachusetts is a famous race in the United States.
- Paul Tergat ran the fastest marathon in 2003. He ran it in two hours, four minutes, and fifty-five seconds!

Wheelchair Racing

Some athletes race in wheelchairs.
They compete in marathons and
other races.
Wheelchair racers have powerful arms.
Their strong hands turn the
wheels quickly.
Wheelchair racers work hard to train.
They race in wheelchairs that are specially
built to be light and fast.

Weird Facts

- The marathon is an event in the Summer Paralympics. The Paralympics are elite sporting events for athletes with disabilities.

- The Boston Marathon has a wheelchair division.

Swimming

Races can also take place in water.
Swimmers race in large pools.
They also race in lakes, rivers, and oceans.
Some races are short contests of speed.
Other races can be over ten miles long!
Swimmers have lean bodies
and strong muscles.
Their powerful arms and legs move
them through the water.

Weird Facts

- There are four different strokes in swimming races: the backstroke, the breaststroke, the butterfly, and the freestyle.

- Most swimmers swim the front crawl for their freestyle stroke.

Bicycle Race

The most famous bicycle race in the world
is called the *Tour de France*.
It lasts for 23 days.
Each day, there is a new race.
The bicycle racer with the fastest times
of all the races wins.
Racers ride over 2,000 miles through France
and its surrounding countries.

Weird Facts

- The best climber in each Tour de France wears a red polka dot jersey.
- The Tour de France is similar to running a marathon almost every day for three weeks!

Triathlon

The triathlon is one of the toughest races
in the world.
The race is made up of three parts.
Racers swim 2.4 miles.
They bike 112 miles.
Then, they run a full marathon,
which is 26.2 miles!
Triathlon racers must be good
at all three sports.
They swim, bike, and run for miles each week
to get ready for the event.

Weird Facts

- In most triathlons, the three events are back-to-back. A racer's time includes the time it takes to change clothes and shoes.
- The Ironman® World Championship is a famous triathlon in Hawaii.

Snowboard Racing

Snowboard racers surf down
snow-covered mountains.
Sometimes, the racing slope is steep and icy.
Each racer rushes down the slope alone.
The racer makes wide, fast turns.
Poles called *gates* mark where
the racer should turn.
If a racer misses just one gate,
he or she is out of the race.
The racer with the fastest time wins.

Weird Facts

- Snowboarding became an Olympic sport in 1998.
- At the 2004 Winter Olympics, American snowboarders won seven medals.

Motocross

Motocross is a motorcycle race
on a dirt track.
The racers ride motorcycles that are
very light but very tough.
They race through ruts and thick mud.
Motocross racers must use skill and
careful planning.
They plan how to pass other racers.
One small mistake, and they could wreck
and lose the race.

Weird Facts

- Motocross is sometimes called *MX* or *MotoX*.
- Motocross racers wear lots of safety equipment, including a helmet, goggles, boots, and plastic guards for their shins, knees, and elbows.

Stock Car Racing

Stock car racing is a sport of speed
and danger.
Drivers must have great skill.
They drive cars around a racetrack
at over 160 miles per hour.
They speed only inches from the other cars.
If a driver loses control, it could mean
a deadly crash.

Weird Facts

- *NASCAR* stands for the "National Association for Stock Car Auto Racing." It began in 1948.

- Stock cars used for racing are specially made. Each one costs millions of dollars to build!

Indy Car Racing

Indy cars are different from stock cars.
Indy cars have "wings" at the front
and back.
They help the car move faster.
The driver's seat is also open to the air.
Indy cars race around a racetrack at
speeds of 200 miles per hour or more.
They get their name from a famous race,
the Indianapolis 500.
This race is 500 miles long!

Weird Facts

- It is tradition for the winner of the Indianapolis 500 to drink milk in the winner's circle.
- Indy car racers go to the track a month ahead of time to do practice laps.

Motorboat Racing

Motorboat racers must be skilled drivers.
Their boats must be in top shape.
Motorboats, called *hydroplanes*, reach speeds
of 200 miles per hour or more.
The racers risk being thrown from the boats.
In some races, the drivers do as many
laps as they can in a set time.
In other races, the drivers go as fast as they
can in a short time.

Weird Facts

- When hydroplane racing first began, it was not uncommon for racers to get hurt or even die. Today, the sport is much safer.

- Some powerful racing boats have four engines.

Yacht Racing

Yachts are fast and graceful on the water.
But racing them in rough seas
can be dangerous.
It takes a skilled team of sailors
to race a yacht.
Sailors can fall overboard, or the yacht
could overturn.
One of the world's most famous yacht
races is called the *America's Cup*.

Weird Facts

- The best boat builders and sailors in the world take part in the America's Cup.
- In 1983, an Australian yacht won the America's Cup. The United States had won the cup for 126 years straight before that.

219

Hot Air Balloon Racing

Hot air balloons may look peaceful
as they float in the sky.
But racing a hot air balloon is not easy.
The pilot must watch the weather carefully.
He or she must pay attention to the wind.
The balloon is very hard to steer.
Strong winds and storms can pull a balloon
off the racecourse and cause a crash.

Weird Facts

- There are over 7,000 hot air balloons in the United States.

- In some races, hot air balloon teams must steer very close to targets on the ground and then drop weights on them.

221

Horse Racing

Racehorses are very powerful, fast animals.
They weigh over 1,000 pounds.
Their hooves sound like thunder
as they run around a racetrack.
Racehorse riders are called *jockeys*.
They know their horses well.
A jockey must be able to control his or her
horse during the race.
A fall from a racehorse could be deadly.

Weird Facts

- The Triple Crown is the most famous prize for horse races in America.

- The Triple Crown is made up of three races: the Kentucky Derby, the Preakness, and the Belmont Stakes.

Sled Dog Racing

In sled dog racing, people and animals race together.
The driver of the sled is called a *musher*.
The musher's team of dogs pulls the sled throughout the race.
The Iditarod is the world's most famous sled dog race.
It takes place in Alaska each year.
Mushers and their teams of dogs race on icy, snowy trails for days and days.

Weird Facts

- The Iditarod is over 1,000 miles long. It takes more than a week, sometimes two weeks, to complete it.

- If a musher gets hurt or stuck during an Iditarod, other mushers always stop to help.

ULTIMATE! Races
Comprehension Questions

1. What is a race?

2. How long is a marathon?

3. Why do you think wheelchair racers have powerful arms?

4. Name four places swimmers can race.

5. What is the name of the most famous bicycle race in the world? How long does it last?

6. What three events make up a triathlon?

7. Where do snowboard racers compete?

8. Which is faster: Stock car racing or Indy car racing?

9. How many miles long is the Indianapolis 500?

10. How can yacht racing be dangerous?

11. Who are jockeys?

Guided Reading Level: K

THRILLING!
Sports

By Teresa Domnauer

Table of Contents

Extreme sports are different from other sports.
The athletes are daring.
They train hard and have special skills.
They do things other people would be
afraid to do.
Extreme sports may look a little wild.
But they are an exciting challenge
for many people around the world.

Skateboarding

Extreme skateboarders like to "get air."
They practice tricks, or stunts, in skate parks.
Skate parks have curved ramps
and smooth bowl-shaped ramps.
Skateboarders zoom up the ramps
and take off into the air.
They fly and flip and twist.
After a jump, a good skateboarder lands on
the board and keeps rolling!

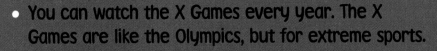

Weird Facts

- You can watch the X Games every year. The X Games are like the Olympics, but for extreme sports.

- In skateboarding, a fall is called a *bail*. Skateboarders wear helmets and pads to protect their bodies.

Snowboarding

Freestyle snowboarders do amazing tricks.
They flip and turn in the air, just like
skateboarders do.
Ski areas have special parks
where snowboarders can practice.
There, they take turns in the halfpipe.
The halfpipe is a valley cut in the snow.
Snowboarders launch high into the air
from the sides of the halfpipe.

Weird Facts

- In 1998, snowboarding became part of the Winter Olympic Games.

- Another kind of snowboarding is called *freeriding*. Freeriders race down steep trails and jump off high mountain cliffs.

233

Free Skiing

Some skiers ski where no others have before.
These skiers are called *free skiers*.
Some free skiers climb to the top
of jagged mountain peaks.
Others fly to the top in helicopters.
Then, they race down the mountain
at high speeds.
If they come to a cliff, they jump off, land,
and keep going.

Weird Facts

- Free skiers who climb up mountains and then ski down them are called *ski mountaineers.*

- Sometimes, free skiers are up to their hips in powdery snow as they ski!

Surfing

Surfers spend a lot of time in the ocean.
They travel the world looking for
the biggest waves.
Surfers paddle out into the ocean.
When the right wave comes, they "pop up,"
or stand quickly, on their surfboards.
Sometimes, the waves are over ten feet high!
If surfers aren't careful, the waves will
crash over them.
The powerful waves can knock them
under the water.

Weird Facts

- Athletes who ride extremely large, high waves are called *big-wave surfers*. They ride waves over 40 feet high!

- Some of the best places to surf are in Hawaii, Indonesia, Australia, and California.

Whitewater Kayaking

Some kayakers paddle in calm lakes or ponds.
Not whitewater kayakers.
They like the thrill of wild,
fast-moving water.
Whitewater kayakers must paddle quickly.
They dodge sharp rocks as rushing water
pushes them downstream.
Whitewater kayakers wear helmets
and life jackets to stay safe.

Weird Facts

- Eskimo first made kayaks from wood and animal bones and skins.

- Kayakers do an "Eskimo roll" if they get stuck upside-down under water. They use their paddles to turn the kayak right side up.

Motocross

Motocross riders do not race on the street.
They race powerful motorcycles
on tough courses made of dirt.
They zoom over hills and through ruts.
They dodge tree stumps and rocks.
They race through muddy puddles.
Motocross racers must be aware of
other riders, too.
Racers don't want to crash into each other.

Weird Facts

- Freestyle motocross riders do tricks in the air, just like skateboarders do. Some can even do back flips!

- To protect their bodies, motocross racers wear special body armor, goggles, and helmets.

241

BMX

BMX is a short way to say
"bicycle motocross."
Instead of motorcycles,
BMX riders use special bicycles.
Freestyle BMX riders perform stunts.
These riders take to the air.
In skate parks, they launch off ramps.
They bounce off rails.
They fly high through the air and flip.
They land again in the riding position.

Weird Facts

- BMX bikes are smaller and lower than most bikes. They have knobby tires that grip the ground.

- BMX riders wear helmets and pads to protect their bodies in case of falls.

Snocross

Some people race snowmobiles.
This sport is called *snocross*.
A lot of snow is needed for snocross racing.
Racers often face heavy snowstorms
that make it hard to see.
A snocross course is icy and bumpy.
The narrow trails twist and turn.
Drivers must steer around huge holes
without crashing.

- Snocross snowmobiles can go from 0 to 70 miles per hour in about 4 seconds!

- Snowmobiles weigh twice as much as motocross motorcycles. Even so, freestyle snocross drivers can do tricks in the air!

245

Rock Climbing

Rock climbers aren't afraid of heights.
They climb steep rocks.
They move one leg or arm at a time.
Each grip they have on the rock
is called a *hold*.
They test each hold before they move.
Sometimes, rock climbers cannot find a hold.
Then, they must move sideways before they can go up.
Ropes secure rock climbers in case they fall.

Weird Facts

- Some rock climbers climb without ropes or other people. This is called *free solo climbing*. This can be very dangerous.

- Moving back down a rock using ropes is called *rappelling*.

Ice Climbing

Ice climbing is a lot like rock climbing.
But ice climbers face freezing-cold weather.
They scale frozen waterfalls.
They climb big sheets of ice called *glaciers*.
Ice climbers wear spikes on their boots.
The spikes help them grip the ice.
Ice climbers carry special tools, too.
They pound axes into the ice
to help pull themselves up.

Weird Facts

- Ice climbers must not climb when the weather is too warm. The ice gets slippery and can crack!

- Ice climbers wear special clothing that is both warm and waterproof.

Skydiving

Skydivers ride high into the air in airplanes.
Then, they jump out!
Skydivers wear parachutes on their backs.
At the right time, they open the parachutes.
The parachutes catch air and let them
float for a while before landing.
Some skydivers jump in a group.
They hold onto each other as they fall.

Weird Facts

- Skydivers always wear two parachutes in case one does not work.
- Skydivers must take lessons on the ground before they go up in a plane.

Bungee Jumping

Bungee jumpers do not jump from planes.
They jump from tall cliffs or high bridges.
Bungee jumpers attach a special cord
to one ankle.
The other end attaches to the cliff or bridge.
A bungee cord is like a big, strong rubber band.
It stretches as the jumper falls.
It is just long enough to keep
the jumper from hitting the ground.

Weird Facts

- South Africa has one of the highest bridges for bungee jumping. It is over 700 feet tall!

- A.J. Hackett started one of the first bungee jumping companies in 1988 in New Zealand.

254

Sled Dog Racing

In Alaska, sled dog racing is an extreme sport.
The Iditarod is a challenging sled dog race.
The race is about 1,200 miles long.
It usually takes about two weeks to finish.
It passes through frozen, snowy lands.
The racers are called *mushers*.
Each musher leads a team of dogs
that pulls a sled.
The mushers must carry supplies and take
care of the dogs along the tough racing route.

Weird Facts

- The Iditarod race takes about two weeks to finish. It is the longest sled dog race in the world.

- Mushers often put special booties on their dogs' feet to protect them from the cold.

THRILLING! Sports
Comprehension Questions

1. How are extreme sports different from other sports?

2. What do you think it means to "get air"?

3. What is a halfpipe? What extreme sport uses a halfpipe?

4. Where do motocross riders race?

5. What does *BMX* stand for?

6. What is it called when people race snowmobiles?

7. Why do you think rock climbers are not afraid of heights?

8. Why do ice climbers wear spikes on their boots?

9. Why do skydivers wear parachutes on their backs?

10. What is the Iditarod? How long does it usually take to complete?

11. Which of these extreme sports would you most like to try? Which would you least like to try?